WEIRD WILDLIFE

SEA CREATURES

Clare Oliver

Raintree

Chicago, Illinois

LOOK FOR THE DOLPHIN

Look for the dolphin in boxes like this. Here you will find extra facts, stories, and other interesting information about sea creatures.

Published by Raintree, a division of Reed Elsevier, Inc.

Designer: Tessa Barwick
Editors: Jason Hook, Pam Wells
Consultant: Joyce Pope

Library of Congress Cataloging-in-Publication Data
Oliver, Clare.
  Sea Creatures / Clare Oliver.
    p. cm.—(Weird wildlife)
  Includes bibliographical references (p.).
  Summary: Discusses various sea creatures and how they live, including slugs, jellies, sharks, dolphins, and whales.

  ISBN 0-7398-4859-3 (HC),
  1-4109-0081-9 (Pbk.)
    1. Marine animals—Juvenile literature.
[1. Marine animals.] I. Title. II. Series.

QLI22.2 .054 2002
591.77—dc21   2001034939

Printed in Hong Kong.
1 2 3 4 5 6 7 8 9 0 LB 05 04 03 02 01

Acknowledgments
We wish to thank the following individuals and organizations for their help and assistance and for supplying material in their collections: Bruce Coleman Collection 2 (Tony Karacsonyi), 4 (Franco Banfi), 6 bottom (Jim Watt), 12 bottom (Tony Karacsonyi), 16 (Jim Watt), 19 top (C&S Hood), 21 (Pacific Stock); Corbis 1 (Jeffrey L Rotman), 3 (Robert Yin), 5 top (Jeffrey L Rotman), 5 bottom (Jeffrey L Rotman), 6 top (Lawson Wood), 7 (Brandon D Cole), 17 (Jeffrey L Rotman), 22 (W Perry Conway), 24 top (Bruce Robinson), 24 bottom (Jeffrey L Rotman), 26 (Robert Yin), 27 (Jeffrey L Rotman); FLPA 20 top (Minden Pictures); MPM Images 8-9, 9 right, 12 top, 28, 29, 30, 31; NHPA front cover (ANT), back cover top (Norbert Wu), back cover bottom left (Trevor McDonald), 10 (Norbert Wu), 11 top (ANT), 13 (ANT), 14 (Image Quest 3-D), 15 (Trevor McDonald); Oxford Scientific Films back cover bottom right (Norbert Wu), 9 left (Karen Gowlett-Holmes), 11 bottom (Rudie Kuiter), 18 (Rodger Jackman), 19 bottom (Howard Hall), 20 bottom (Daniel J Cox), 23 (Daniel J Cox), 25 (Norbert Wu).

▼ One of the most dangerous sea creatures is the blue-ringed octopus. It may only be about 6 inches (15 cm) across, but it contains enough venom to kill a human. See page 12.

▶ The cuttlefish has a strange trick for confusing its enemies. It can squirt out clouds of dark inky liquid. Find out more on page 26.

CONTENTS

SEA CREATURES

**Sea creatures live in all parts of the ocean—
shallow and deep, icy and warm. They range
from monster mammals to tiny creatures
that are too small to see without a microscope.**

▼ Check out the
whale shark's huge,
gaping mouth!
Inside are 300 rows
of tiny teeth.

There are all kinds of fish. The smallest, the dwarf goby,
would fit on your fingertip. The largest, the whale shark,
weighs as much as six elephants. Strangely, the giant
whale shark's diet includes some of the ocean's tiniest
creatures. These are called plankton.

◄ Lizards are the largest family
of reptiles. Chameleons,
geckos, iguanas and skinks are
all types of lizards.

The ocean is home to reptiles, such as turtles and sea snakes. There are also creatures, like lobsters and crabs, with shells as hard as armor but no skeletons. Other sea creatures have soft bodies and no armor. They include octopuses that can change color and squirt clouds of black ink, sea anemones that look like flowers, and starfish covered in thorns.

Oceans cover two-thirds of Earth's surface and stretch down deeper than the tallest mountains. There are probably more weird sea creatures that we have not even discovered yet.

▲ A crown-of-thorns starfish munches on some coral. Starfish have gobbled up whole sections of the Great Barrier Reef off Australia.

 HUGE SQUIDS

The giant squid grows to over 59 feet (18 m) long. It also has no bones! The squid's huge, bullet-shaped body with eight arms and two tentacles that stretch make it an expert mover—and it can move backward too!

▶ The giant Pacific octopus is the largest octopus in the world. It can grow up to 31 feet (9.6 m) from arm tip to arm tip.

FREAKY FISH

Believe it or not, there is no such thing as a standard "fish" shape! The oceans are home to fish of just about every shape and size that you can imagine.

▼ Garden eels are strange fish that bury their bodies in the seabed. Their top halves wave around in the current picking up food or duck down when danger approaches.

FISH SHOCK

Electric rays use a stun gun to catch their prey! These fish can cover themselves with a cloak of electricity. If a creature swims into the electric cloak, it is stunned by the shock!

Eels are fish that look more like snakes. In warm waters, tiny garden eels pop up and down from burrows in the seabed. In cold, deep waters, snipe eels snap up shrimp in jaws that look like beaks.

Flying fish have fins that look like wings. They use these fins to leap out of the water and glide through the air. Fish called rays are shaped like kites and seem to fly underwater when they flap their fins. Some rays have a secret weapon—a tail that can give attackers a painful sting.

◄ Manta rays are huge but harmless—even though they are related to sharks. From wingtip to wingtip they may measure as much as 20 feet (6 m).

Hagfish look like eels with no jaws. These ugly mugs burrow their way into the skin of dead or dying fish, eating the flesh as they go. Their other tricks include tying themselves in knots and producing loads of slime.

The hagfish's tiny teeth are perfect for gnawing bits of fish flesh. Four feelers around the mouth help the hagfish find its food.

CORAL REEF

Colorful coral reefs grow in warm, shallow waters. They are built from the skeletons of millions of tiny animals called corals. The corals grow in all sorts of weird shapes. Some look like broccoli, while others look like brains!

▼ One reef may be home to as many as 350 different corals. The amazing shapes they form provide millions of hiding places for the other reef creatures.

Beautiful, rainbow-colored fish live among the coral. There are blue parrotfish, yellow angelfish, and orange-and-white clownfish. Clownfish swim around among the deadly stinging tentacles of one type of sea anemone. For some mysterious reason, the clownfish do not get stung by this one type. But any enemies chasing them do!

The boxer crab carries a small anemone in each pincer. These "boxing gloves" pack a stinging punch!

Many other strange creatures live on the reef. Giant clams are shellfish with a shell so big that a baby could take a bath in it. Clams are filter feeders. That means they catch the small plankton as they take in a mouthful of water. Then they spit out the water, leaving just the plankton to swallow.

▲ A cleaner wrasse grazes on the face of a grouper fish. The wrasse gets a free meal, and the grouper gets cleaned up.

A TRIP TO THE BARBERS

Small fish called cleaner wrasse seem to like danger. They swim into the mouths of fierce hunting fish, such as groupers and moray eels. They do this to get at the tiny creatures that live on the fish scales and to clean their teeth, too. Cleaner wrasse are also called barber fish.

WORLD OF WEEDS

Underwater forests of kelp and other types of seaweed are near the shore. These provide food for some sea creatures and a hiding place for others.

▼ Sea otters live in the North Pacific. They do not have blubber to keep their bodies warm. Instead, they have denser fur than any other mammal.

Sea otters gather up mussels and other shellfish that live around the kelp. Then they use stones they've carried up from the seabed to crack open the mussels on their chest. Otters also twist strands of weeds around themselves, so that they can take a nap without being washed out to sea!

◄ A chameleon's toes are ridged soles with that are like cling film. They grip so well that the lizard can climb sheer walls and even run across the ceiling upside-down!

The most elegant creatures among the weeds are the seahorses and leafy sea dragons. They may look weird and have strange names, but these creatures are actually fish. Leafy sea dragons look just like floating pieces of seaweed. This disguise helps them hide from hungry hunters who might want to eat them.

▲ Can you see the eggs under this male leafy sea dragon's tail? He will guard them until they hatch.

PREGNANT DAD

Seahorses are mixed-up parents. The dad, not the mom, keeps the growing babies in his belly. When he gives birth, hundreds of tiny seahorses stream out into the ocean.

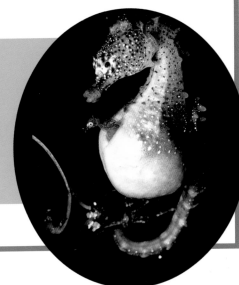

11

POISON

Many sea creatures use poison as a weapon. Some use it to defend themselves against bigger creatures. Others use poison to kill or stun their prey.

▲ The stonefish lies on the seabed in warm, shallow waters and looks just like a stone. Beware of stepping on one, though. It has spines tipped with enough venom to kill you.

The Belcher's sea snake has the most deadly bite of any snake on land or in the sea. Its fangs inject superstrong poison into its prey. Luckily, this fierce creature attacks fish rather than people.

▲ The blue-ringed octopus lives off the coast of Australia.

The blue-ringed octopus may look too small and pretty to be dangerous, but its bite can kill a person in just a few minutes.

▼ Pufferfish swallow lots of air or water to puff up their bodies and show off their spines. If the spines don't scare off a predator, a tiny taste of the fish's poisonous flesh sure will!

The octopus's spit contains the same poison that is found in the organs of the deadly pufferfish. The pufferfish has a smooth body, until it senses danger. Then it puffs itself up, and its spikes stick out of its skin, turning the fish into a prickly ball.

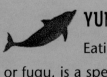

YUM! YUM!
Eating pufferfish, or fugu, is a special treat in Japan. People who eat fugu like to have a tiny taste of the poison. It adds to the flavor— and numbs the mouth!

SLUGS AND JELLYFISH

The sea is home to all kinds of floppy, rubbery creatures that would have no chance of moving around on land. The water supports their weight and lets them float freely.

Jellyfish are just like wobbly, see-through jelly. They come in shades of pink and blue and look like something you might find in a candy store. Jellyfish have a round body, called the bell, and a mass of trailing tentacles, or feelers, that can sting. The most dangerous is the box jellyfish, nicknamed the "sea wasp." It has about 60 tentacles, each covered with millions of stingers, that together hold enough poison to kill a person.

◀ A jellyfish drifts along, with its tentacles trailing. The camera flash has made the jellyfish look pink, but really its body is blue.

The Spanish dancer is one of the most dazzling sea creatures. It is a type of sea slug and gets its name from its gills. These are feathery and fan out like a flamenco dancer's dress. The beautiful Spanish dancers can be red, pink, yellow, or blue.

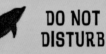

DO NOT DISTURB

The Spanish dancer spends much of its time crawling slowly along the seabed, grazing on sea sponges. But if it is disturbed, it suddenly takes off and swims through the water with its colorful gills flapping on either side of its body like wings

◄ A pair of sea slugs off the coast of Indonesia. Colorful sea slugs are found only in warm waters.

KILLER SHARKS

The great hunters of the sea are the sharks, and the scariest of them all is the great white shark. Its body is shaped like a bullet and packed with muscle. This means the great white can race through the water at over 30 kph.

Nearly all fish, including most sharks, are cold-blooded. But the great white shark is slightly warm-blooded, so its warm muscles can power it through the cold water even faster. The great white's mouth has rows of jagged teeth, and its jaws have enough biting power to bend a steel bar. The great white sometimes attacks people. These attacks often have serious results.

◀ The scary, gaping mouth of a great white shark.

The tiger shark is another vicious killer. This greedy monster will eat just about anything, from fish to people. One tiger shark washed up on a beach was found to have a whole suit of armor in its belly!

▼ On each end of the "hammer," the hammerhead shark has a nostril as well as an eye. That means it can sniff both ways, too!

HAMMER HORROR

The hammerhead shark has a really weird head. It is T-shaped, like the head of a hammer. With its eyes goggling from the ends of this hammer, the shark can look both ways to find its favorite food – stingrays.

Incredible Travelers

Some sea creatures travel amazing distances as the seasons change, or at certain times of their lives. They might want to find warmer water, tastier food, or a place to breed.

Some animals that make long journeys spend only part of their life in the sea. Freshwater eels live and feed in rivers but breed in the warm waters of the Sargasso Sea in the north Atlantic Ocean. The tiny baby eels travel more than 3,400 miles (5,500 km) across the ocean. It is a mystery how they find their way.

▼ Elvers, or baby eels, swim together from the Sargasso, but they will live alone as adults.

Female loggerhead turtles are also amazing travelers. They may journey 6,200 miles (10,000 km) to find the right place to lay their eggs. The loggerheads travel back to the beach where they were born. Then, they come ashore and bury their leathery eggs in the sand.

◀ Strong flippers power this green turtle through the water. Females come ashore to lay eggs every three years.

WONDER WINGS

Creatures of the air, not the sea, make the longest journeys. Arctic terns are sea birds that can lay their eggs in the Far North of the world, but they may travel to the Far South when winter comes. In a lifetime, the tern flies far enough to have gone to the moon and back!

Spiny lobsters make their long journeys in single file like soldiers. Nobody knows why they march over the seabed in a row, but it means that the leader shields all the other lobsters from the ocean currents. The lobsters may travel for 31 miles (50 km), with some 50 lobsters in each line.

▲ Spiny lobsters journey to deeper waters each autumn, where they can escape winter storms.

DOLPHINS AND WHALES

Among the most playful creatures in the sea are the dolphins. They are famous for being intelligent and friendly to humans. Dolphins have even rescued people who were drowning.

But killer whales are also members of the dolphin family. They are ferocious hunters, with a taste for baby seals. When they catch one, they don't gulp it down right away. First, killer whales play a strange game with the seals, tossing them up into the air.

The narwhal and the beluga look a bit like dolphins and belong to the whale group. They live in the icy Arctic Ocean and have a weird and wonderful appearance. The male narwhal looks a little like a unicorn from a fairy tale. It has a tall spiral tooth, up to 10 feet (3 m) long, like a horn that points out from its head. The beluga is the only all-white whale. Perhaps its pale coloring helps to disguise it when it swims among the icebergs.

▼ Beluga calves are dark gray. The whales fade to white only when they are about four years old.

SWEET WHALE MUSIC

Many whales sing and call to one another, and the beluga has the sweetest song of all. It has been nicknamed the "sea canary" because of the twittering noises it makes.

GIANT OF THE OCEANS

▼ The hole on top of a blue whale's head is called a blowhole. When the whale comes up to the surface to breathe out, a cloud of misty water blows out of the hole.

The biggest ocean creature, and also the biggest animal on Earth, is the blue whale. This mighty mammal can grow as long as 18 tall divers swimming head to toe and can weigh more than 25 elephants.

The blue whale is so huge that you could crawl through one of its blood vessels with room to spare. Its heart is as big as a small family car. It is not only the largest animal, but also the noisiest. When a blue whale calls, the sound can be heard hundreds of miles away. It is louder than a jet engine and sounds like low grunts!

Blue whales eat tiny shellfish, called krill, and devour 4 tons of the stuff in a single day. They feed by gulping in huge amounts of water. Their amazing, folded throat stretches out to hold it all. Then, the water is forced out through fringed plates made from a material called baleen. The baleen plates act like a sieve to catch pieces of food.

CUTE CALVES

Blue whales give birth to the biggest babies on the planet. A newborn blue whale calf is as long as five divers stretched head to toe. Like all baby mammals, the calf drinks creamy milk—up to 132 pounds (90 kg) every day!

▼ The humpback whale is another baleen whale. Even though it weighs about 30 tons, it can leap completely out of the water! This is called breaching.

SPOOKY DEPTHS

In the depths of the ocean, the waters are ice-cold and horribly dark. These spooky waters are home to the weirdest sea creatures of all.

The deep-sea anglerfish got its name because of its skill at fishing. Above its mouth is a long, thin fin shaped like a fishing rod, with a glowing blob at the end. When small fish come to see if the blob is a tasty worm, the anglerfish gobbles them up.

▲ There are more than 100 different types of anglerfish, and many have pointed spines. The one thing they all have in common is the fishing-rod lure over their mouth.

▶ These strange-looking creatures are called tubeworms. Some types of tubeworms are able to live on the deep ocean floor.

The black swallower is another weird fish that hunts in the gloom. It is only 10 inches (25 cm) long, but somehow it eats meals that are much bigger than its own body! The swallower sinks its teeth into its victim and slowly bites its way along the victim's body. The swallower's belly stretches until everything fits in.

The viperfish has a hunting trick of its own. The fish waits with its mouth open, but its long, see-through fangs are invisible in the dark. When a shrimp swims into the mouth of the viperfish, it slams its jaws shut and the fangs form a cage.

▼ Cookiecutters come to the surface at night but swim to a depth of about 6,562 feet (2,000 m) during the day. Their sharp teeth have taken chunks out of dolphins and even parts of submarines!

BEAMING BELLY

Cookiecutter sharks have "glow-in-the-dark" bellies. They got their name because when they bite their victims, they pull out round plugs of flesh shaped like cookies.

FACTS ABOUT SEA CREATURES

Here are some interesting facts and figures about sea creatures.

Egg explosion
The ocean sunfish lays more eggs than any other fish—well over 300 million in a lifetime.

Chief reef
The Great Barrier Reef, off the northeast coast of Australia, is more than 1,242 miles (2,000 km) long. That makes it the biggest object ever built by living creatures.

A "bed" of clams
A group of clams is called a "bed." A large group of fish is called a "shoal."

Funny flesh
Little is known about the Greenland shark—except that its flesh is poisonous. Eating it makes dogs called huskies act very strangely.

Eye eye
The giant squid has the biggest eyes of any living creature. Each one is about 20 inches (50 cm) across—twice as big as a dinner plate.

Tremendous tentacles
The largest octopus is the giant Pacific octopus that has tentacles that stretch out about 8.2 feet (2.5 m).

▼ Cuttlefish have pockets of gas inside their bodies. They can change the amount of gas in order to sink down in the water or float upward.

Color codes

Cuttlefish, octopuses, and squid can all change color. They do this to send messages to a mate, to disguise themselves from creatures hunting them, or to creep up on their own prey.

Star turn

When starfish have their arms bitten off, they are able to grow new ones as long as the central disc of the body is still there. Some starfish can even grow a new body from a tiny bit of arm.

Crazy crabs

The Japanese spider crab is the biggest crab, with legs that stretch more than 11 feet (3.5 m). The smallest crab is the pea crab that lives inside the shells of oysters and mussels and is about the size of a pea.

Mr. and Mrs.

Some female deep-sea anglerfish grow to more than 3.3 feet (1 m) long. Male anglerfish can be less than 2.3 inches (6 cm) long.

Smiling shark

The great white shark's jaws open to 3.3 feet (1 m) wide. They contain sets of teeth that are replaced about every six weeks—no wonder, with all the hard work they do.

▲ Named for their spidery legs, spider crabs are found in just about all the oceans. This one is in the Caribbean Sea.

Full sail ahead

A race across the ocean would be won by the sailfish, which can speed along at 68 miles (109 kmh). Sailfish are shaped to cut through the water, with pointed noses and long, smooth bodies.

Mighty manta

The biggest rays are manta rays. They have wings stretching 23 feet (7 m) across and weigh around 2,976 pounds (1,350 kg).

Whale ways

Gray whales and humpbacks journey farther than any other mammals. They travel distances of 9,942 miles (16,000 km) or more every year.

Penguins at their own pace

Penguins are birds that swim instead of flying. They have flippers, not wings. The fastest swimmers are emperor penguins. They reach speeds of nearly 9 miles per hour (15 kmh).

▲ Fish like snapper swim in large groups called shoals, or schools.

Words About Sea Creatures

This glossary explains some words used in this book that you might not have seen before.

baleen (BAY-leen)
The material that some whales have in the roof of their mouths that they use to sieve food out of the water. It can be fringed or in a single plate hanging from the roof of the whale's mouth. Baleen varies from whale to whale.

breed (breed)
Produce young, or babies.

cold-blooded (BLUD-id)
Having blood that changes temperature depending on the surrounding temperature. Most fish are cold-blooded, so the temperature of their blood is about the same as the ocean's.

coral reef (KOR-uhl reef)
An underwater structure, made of the skeletons of tiny creatures called corals.

currents (KUR-uhntz)
Movements of water that can affect the movements of sea creatures.

fish
A group of animals that live underwater, are covered in scales, and breathe through slits called gills.

flamenco (fluh-MEN-ko)
A Spanish dance in which the female dancers wear colorful, flowing dresses.

gills (gilz)
The feathery things that lie beneath the gill covers on the side of a fish's head. Gills allow fish to breathe by taking oxygen out of the water.

krill (kril)
Shrimplike plankton.

mammals (MAM-uhlz)
A group of warm-blooded animals. They have a backbone, breathe air, and feed their young on the mother's milk. Whales and seals are mammals that live in the ocean.

muscles (MUHSS-uhlz)
The parts inside a body that stretch and contract to allow an animal to move.

plankton (PLANGK-tuhn)
Tiny plants and animals that float in water, often near the surface. They are carried by the ocean currents.

prey (pray)
An animal that is hunted and killed by another animal for food.

reptiles (REP-tilz)
A group of cold-blooded animals that have a bony skeleton and scaly skin. Reptiles include snakes, turtles, crocodiles, and lizards.

Sargasso Sea (sar-GAH-soh)
A part of the Atlantic Ocean, where the water is thick with seaweed.

shellfish (SHEL-fish)
Sea creatures that have no skeleton but have tough shells to protect their soft bodies. Crabs and lobsters are types of shellfish.

sponge (SPUNJ)
A sea creature found on the bottom of the ocean. Its dead body is used by bathers because it can hold so much water.

tentacles (TEN-tuh-kuhlz)
A creature's long feelers that bend and are used for sensing things, moving around, catching prey, or stinging.

warm-blooded (worm-BLUD-id)
Having warm blood that does not change temperature, even if the sea or air changes temperature. Humans and seals are warm-blooded creatures.

▶ Sponges, like these purple tube sponges, are very simple animals. Long ago people thought they were a type of plant.

PROJECTS ABOUT SEA CREATURES

WATER'S EDGE REPORT

Next time you visit the seashore, have a close look at a shallow pool of water. You may find relatives of some of the creatures you have read about in this book, such as starfish, anemones, sponges, or crabs. To make a report, draw pictures of what you see. Then, write about what the creatures do. Always tell an adult where you are going. Be careful not to slip on slimy seaweed or slippery rocks. If you live far from the seashore, visit a local aquarium instead.

▼ Male humpback whales sing the longest songs. Each can last more than 30 minutes.

WHALE MUSIC

Why not visit your local library and borrow recordings of whales singing. How many different types of noise can you hear? Some sounds are like deep groans, while others are more like squawks. See how long a song lasts before the whale starts at the beginning again. Listen to different recordings until you start to know the type of whale by the noises it makes. Can you tell the difference between a blue whale and a humpback whale? Can you find a musical instrument that makes a noise like a whale's song?

MAKE A CORAL REEF GAME

On a large piece of oaktag, draw lots of different types of fish you could find on a coral reef. Cut them out and color them in. On the blank side, write the name of the fish to help you remember it. Also write a score of 1, 2, or 5 on each fish.

Decorate the inside of a shoe box to look like a coral reef. Then attach a paper clip to each fish and scatter them all inside the box, with the colored side facing up. Tie a small magnet to a piece of string to make a fishing rod. Take turns with a friend to fish. When all the fish have been caught, add up the scores to see who has won.

SEA CREATURES ON THE WEB

If you have access to the Internet, try looking up these websites:

Enchanted Learning
www.enchantedlearning.com/subjects/sharks/
This brilliant site has loads of great information about sharks.

Marine Life Learning Center
www.fishid.com
This is the home page of the Marine Life Learning Center website. The site includes bright fishy photo quizzes, with pictures of beautiful coral reef fish for you to name.

▲ Look at pictures of colorful coral reefs like this one, before you decorate your coral reef game.

Dolphin Log
www.dolphinlog.org/creatures.htm
Check out photos and features on dolphins, turtles, sea dragons, and other animals.

Gallery of Deep Ocean Creatures
www.extremescience.com/deepcreat.htm
Meet some creepy deep-sea monsters and find out all about how animals glow in the dark. Explore the rest of the site to find record-breaking marine animals, such as the giant squid.

Sea Slug Forum
www.seaslugforum.net/hexasang.htm
This page has lots of information about Spanish dancers, including photos of them "dancing." Explore the links and the rest of the site to find out about other stunning sea slugs.

INDEX